Illustrated by Simone Abel

Educational consultant: Rhona Whiteford

BROCKHAMPTON PRESS

one cat

2

two children

3

three bears

4

four babies

5

five dogs

6

six shoes

7

seven aeroplanes

8

eight mice

9

nine cars

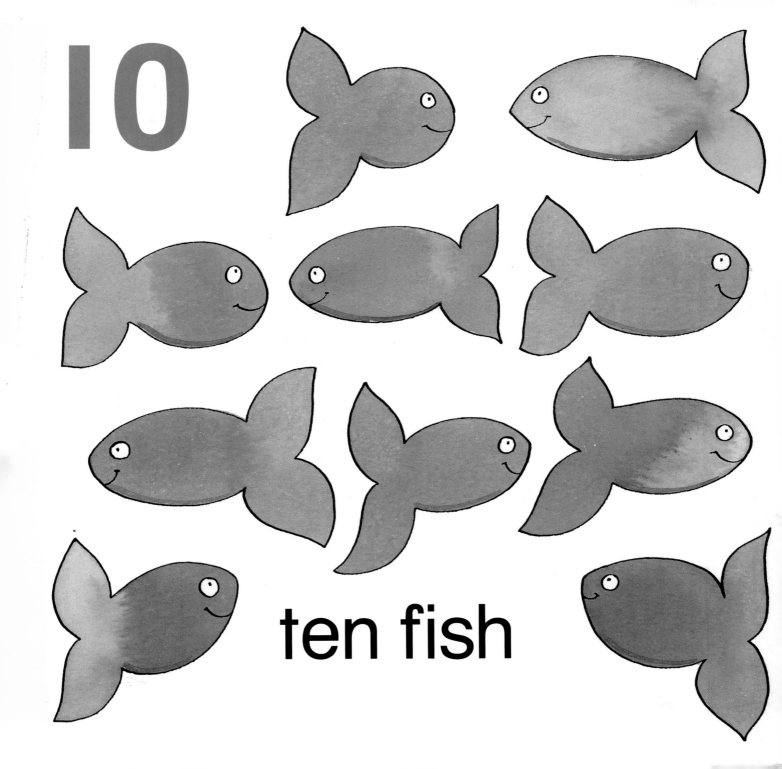

10

ten fish

How many balloons?

How many elephants?

How many bees?

How many candles?

How many ducklings?

How many socks?

How many kittens?

How many flowers?

How many ice-creams?

How many crayons?

What can you count?

This edition published in the United Kingdom
in 2001 by Brockhampton Press
20 Bloomsbury Street, London WC1B 3JH
a member of the Caxton Publishing Group

First published in 1993

© 1993 Hodder Headline

Cover Designed and Produced for Brockhampton Press by Open Door Limited
80 High Street, Colsterworth, Lincolnshire NG33 5JA

Title: 123
ISBN: 1-84186-072-7